Let's Talk About
BEING GREEDY

Let's Talk About
BEING GREEDY

By JOY BERRY

Illustrated by John Costanza
Edited by Kate Dickey
Designed by Abigail Johnston

GROLIER ENTERPRISES CORP.

Let's talk about BEING GREEDY.

Sometimes you need to share something with other people.

It is important to be fair whenever you share.
Sharing is fair when every person takes
his or her **fair share.**

A fair share is the part of something
that a person deserves to have.

Sometimes having a fair share means each person takes the same amount.

Sometimes a fair share is something that a person really needs. Sometimes a fair share is something that a person has worked for and has earned.

Whenever people try to take *more* than their fair share, they are **being greedy.**

Sometimes people are greedy because they *are always dissatisfied*. They are not happy with what they have. They always want more.

Sometimes people are greedy because they *are self-centered*. They care much more about themselves than they care about other people.

Sometimes people are greedy because they *feel superior.*

They feel that they are better than others. They feel that because they are better, they deserve to have more than other people have.

Sometimes people are greedy because they *are not fair.*

They do not care whether or not other people have a fair share.

It is not fun to be around people who
- are always dissatisfied,
- are self-centered,
- feel superior, or
- are not fair.

Thus, most people do not like to be around greedy people.

Because no one wants to be around greedy people, greedy people are often unhappy.

If you want to be happy and you want the people around you to be happy, you will avoid being greedy.

Try not to be greedy. When you need to share, do these things:

- Realize that every person deserves a fair share.
- Decide what everyone's fair share will be *before* you share something.
- Let the people with whom you share things help decide what everyone's fair share should be.
- Ask an adult to help you if you and your friends have a difficult time deciding what everyone's fair share should be.

- Give other people their fair share before you take yours.
- Be satisified with your fair share.
- Do not try to take more.
- Do not complain about what you get.

It is important to treat other people the way you want to be treated. If you do not want people to be greedy, you should not be greedy.